The Awesome Power of Blessing

Richard Brunton

The Awesome Power of Blessing
Published by Richard Brunton
New Zealand

© 2017 Richard Brunton

Second edition

ISBN 978-0-473-38744-0 (Softcover)
ISBN 978-0-473-38745-7 (ePUB)
ISBN 978-0-473-38746-4 (Kindle)

Editing:
Special thanks to
Joanne Wiklund and Andrew Killick
for making the story more readable
than it might otherwise have been!

Production & Typesetting:
Andrew Killick
Castle Publishing Services
www.castlepublishing.co.nz

Cover design:
Paul Smith

Printed in New Zealand

CONTENTS

FOREWORD

I encourage you to read this small book with its powerful message – you will be changed!

It was while Richard Brunton and I were having breakfast one morning that he shared what God had revealed to him about the power of blessing, and I immediately saw the potential for great impact in the lives of others.

I filmed his message to show at our church men's camp. The men present thought it was so good they wanted the whole church to hear it. People began putting it into practice in every area of their lives and we heard amazing testimonies as a result. One businessman reported that his business had gone from 'nothing, to profit' within two weeks. Others were physically healed as they began to bless their bodies.

Other opportunities for this message to be heard

began to open up. I was due to speak at a Gathering of the Generals event (where church pastors come together to learn and be refreshed) in Kenya and Uganda. Richard accompanied me on that trip and took a session on blessing. The message broke through long-buried emptiness and pain. Most of the people in the audience had never been blessed by their fathers and as Richard stood in that role and blessed them, many cried and experienced emotional and spiritual release along with an immediate change in their lives.

Knowing how to bless has impacted my life to the point where I now look for opportunities to bless others in 'word and deed' – through what I say and do. You will enjoy this little book, and if you apply it to your life, your fruitfulness will abound and overflow for the Kingdom of God.

Geoff Wiklund
Geoff Wiklund Ministries,
Chairman, Promise Keepers,
Auckland, New Zealand

God has blessed Richard with a revelation of the power of blessing when it is released on others. I believe that this is a revelation from God for our time.

As Richard lives out his message, this brings an authenticity that people immediately relate to.

This caused us to invite Richard to speak at all our Promise Keepers men's events. The impact was immensely powerful and life-changing for many.

'Blessing' was a topic that reached in and grabbed men's hearts at the Promise Keepers events. There was a massive positive response to this important teaching – blessing, benediction and the power of 'good speaking'. Many of the men had never really received blessing or given it to others. After hearing Richard's message, and reading this book, they received a powerful blessing and were equipped to bless others in the name of the Father, the Son and the Holy Spirit.

I commend Richard and this book on *The Awesome Power of Blessing* as a powerful way of releasing the fullness of God's blessing in our families, our communities and our nation.

Paul Subritzky
National Director, Promise Keepers
Auckland, New Zealand

INTRODUCTION

Everyone loves to hear exciting news – and it's even better when you get to tell it!

When I discovered the value of giving a blessing, it was as if I was the man in the Bible who discovered treasure in a field. I enthusiastically shared my thoughts and experiences with Pastor Geoff Wiklund and he asked me to talk to the men from his church at a camp in February 2015. They were so impressed they wanted the whole church to hear the message.

When I spoke at the church, it happened that Reverend Brian France, of Charisma Christian Ministries, and Paul Subritzky, of Promise Keepers NZ, were attending that day. This resulted in my sharing the message at Charisma in New Zealand and in Fiji, and to the men at Promise Keepers as well. Many took hold of it and immediately began putting it into practice with excellent results. Some commented that they had never before heard teaching on this aspect of the Kingdom of God.

The ministry of blessing seemed to snowball. (Doesn't God say, 'A man's gift will make room for him'?) Towards the end of 2015, I accompanied Pastor Geoff to Kenya and Uganda. He was ministering to hundreds of pastors attending the Gathering of the Generals. This was an annual event where the delegates sought inspiration and support, and Geoff felt that my teaching on blessing would be helpful for them. And so it turned out to be. Not only the pastors, but other speakers from America, Australia and South Africa felt it was a powerful message and encouraged me to do something to reach a wider audience.

I neither wanted to build and maintain a website, nor write an in-depth work when other excellent ones already exist. The message of blessing is very simple – easily put into practice – and I didn't want its simplicity lost in complexity – hence this little book.

I have drawn quotations from *The Power of Blessing*

by Kerry Kirkwood, *The Grace Outpouring: Becoming a People of Blessing* by Roy Godwin and Dave Roberts, *The Father's Blessing* by Frank Hammond, and *The Miracle and Power of Blessing* by Maurice Berquist. I'm sure I've drawn or learnt from other people and other books as well, but over the years it's all got merged together.

Discovering the power of blessing will open up a whole new way of living for anyone who acts upon it. I bless people most days now – believers and unbelievers – in cafés, restaurants, hotels, waiting rooms and even on the street. I have blessed orphans, orphanage staff, an air hostess on a plane, orchards, animals, wallets, businesses and medical conditions. I have had grown men and women weeping on my chest as I have proclaimed a father's blessing over them.

When speaking with unbelievers, I have found that 'May I bless you/your business/your marriage etc?' is less threatening than 'Can I pray for you?' Indeed, this simple approach, expressed with loving concern, led to one of my family members coming to know the love and saving power of Jesus Christ, after years of argument.

I often don't get to witness the outcome, but I have seen enough to know that blessing changes lives. And it has changed mine too.

It is God's nature to bless and, as creatures made in His image, it is in our spiritual DNA as well. The Holy Spirit is waiting for God's people to step out in faith and in the authority that Jesus Christ won for them, in order to transform lives.

I am sure you will find this booklet helpful. Jesus has not left us powerless. Speaking blessings in all kinds of situations is a neglected spiritual grace that has the potential to change your world.

Enjoy.
Richard Brunton

PART ONE:

Why Blessing?

THE INSIGHT

My wife Nicole is New Caledonian and so, of course, that meant I needed to learn to speak French and spend a fair bit of time in her birthplace, Noumea. Although New Caledonia is mainly a Catholic country, it wasn't long before I noticed that many people still had contact with the 'dark side', while also practising their religion. It wasn't uncommon for people to visit a medium, clairvoyant or a *guérisseur* without understanding that they were actually consulting witchcraft.

I remember my wife taking me to visit a young woman in her twenties who had been taken to one of these 'healers', but who, soon after, had ended up in a home for mentally disturbed or depressed people. As I understood she was a Christian, I commanded the demons that had entered her to go, in the name of Jesus Christ. A Catholic priest prayed as well and, between us, this girl was set free and discharged from the institution not long after.

Others professed their Catholic religion and yet openly displayed statues or artefacts of other gods. There was one such man I met who had continual stomach problems. One day I said to him that I believed that if he got rid of the big, fat Buddha that was in front of his house – it was all lit up at night – his stomach problems would cease. In addition, some of the artefacts he had collected needed to go. He resisted – how could these 'dead' things possibly make him sick? After some months I saw him again and asked how his stomach was. Somewhat sheepishly he replied, 'I finally took your advice and got rid of the Buddha. My stomach is fine now.'

On another occasion, I was asked to go to the house of a woman with cancer. Before I began to pray I suggested they get rid of the statues of Buddha in their lounge, which her husband immediately did. As I broke curses off her and commanded demons to leave in the name of Jesus, she described an icy coldness moving up her body from her feet and leaving from her head.

So, against this background, I decided to give a teaching on 'curses' to a prayer group that my wife and I had started in our Noumea apartment. The teaching was based on Derek Prince's body of work (Derek Prince was a renowned twentieth-century Bible teacher). While I was preparing my message in French, I learnt that their word for cursing was *malédiction*, and their word for blessing was *bénédiction*. The root meanings for these words are 'bad speaking' and 'good speaking'.

Formerly, when I compared cursing and blessing, cursing seemed dark, heavy and dangerous, and blessing seemed quite lightweight and benign. I had heard teachings on cursing before, but never on blessing – which probably contributed to my perception. I had also never heard anyone bless another person with real intent and impact. In fact, the extent of a Christian's blessing might be to say, 'Bless you', when someone sneezes, or write 'Blessings' at the end of a letter or email – as if it was almost a habit rather than something intentional.

Later, as I thought on these words, 'malediction' and 'benediction', it occurred to me that if 'bad speaking' was powerful, then 'good speaking' should be at least as powerful and, with God, probably much more powerful!

This revelation, together with other insights that we will talk about later, set me off on a course to discover the *power* of blessing.

THE POWER OF OUR SPEAKING

Not wanting to repeat what many good books have said about the power of our words, I want to give a summary of what I believe is very important in this area.

We know that:

> *Death and life are in the power of the tongue and those who love it, will eat its fruit. (Proverbs 18:21)*

Words contain tremendous power – either positive and constructive, or negative and destructive. Each time we speak words (and even use a particular tone, which adds meaning to the words), we speak either life or death to those who hear us and to ourselves. Further, we know that:

Out of the abundance of the heart the mouth speaks. A good man out of the good treasure of his heart brings forth good things, and an evil man out of the evil treasure brings forth evil things. (Matthew 12:34-35)

Thus, out of a critical heart speaks a critical tongue; from a self-righteous heart, a judgemental tongue; an ungrateful heart, a complaining tongue; and so on. Similarly, lustful hearts bear corresponding fruit. The world is full of negative speaking. The media spews it out day after day. Human nature being what it is, we tend not to speak well over people or situations. It doesn't seem to come naturally to us. We often wait until people are dead before saying nice things about them. However, the 'good treasure' springs out of loving hearts that will speak with a gracious tongue; from peaceful hearts, a reconciling tongue; and so on.

The statement, 'and those who love it, will eat its fruit' suggests we will reap what we sow – be it good or bad. In other words, you will get what you say. What do you think of that?

This is true for all human beings, regardless of whether they have a Christian belief or not. Christians and non-Christians alike can speak words of life – for example, either might say: 'Son, that's a great hut you've built. You could be an excellent builder or an architect one day. Well done.'

However, a born-again Christian has a *new* heart. The Bible puts it that we are 'new creations' (2 Corinthians 5:17). Therefore, as Christians, we should be doing more *good* speaking and less *bad*. We can easily lapse into negativity if we are not careful to guard our hearts and words. Once you begin to consciously think about this, you'll be surprised how often Christians – even unwittingly – curse themselves and others. More about that later.

MOVING FROM GOOD SPEAKING TO BLESSING: OUR CALLING

As Christians, with the life of the Lord Jesus flowing through us, we can go beyond just good speaking – we can speak and impart blessings over people or situations – and indeed we are called to do so. Perhaps blessing is our great calling. Read the following:

> *Be tender-hearted, be courteous; not returning evil for evil or reviling for reviling, but on the contrary blessing, knowing that you were called to this, that you may inherit a blessing. (1 Peter 3:8-9)*

We are called to bless and to receive a blessing.

The first thing God spoke to Adam and Eve was a blessing:

> *Then God blessed them, and God said to them,*

> *'Be fruitful and multiply; fill the earth and sub-*
> *due it…' (Genesis 1:28)*

God blessed them so they could be fruitful. Blessing is an attribute of God – it's what He does! And like God – and from God – we too have the authority and the power to bless others.

Jesus blessed. The last thing He did, even as He was about to ascend to heaven, was to bless His disciples:

> *And He led them out as far as Bethany, and*
> *He lifted up His hands and blessed them. Now*
> *it came to pass, while He blessed them, that*
> *He was parted from them and carried up into*
> *heaven. (Luke 24:50-51)*

Jesus is our role model. He said that we should do the same things He did, in His name. We are designed by God to bless.

WHAT IS CHRISTIAN BLESSING?

In the Old Testament, the word 'blessing' is the Hebrew word *barak*. This simply means, 'to speak the intention of God'.

In the New Testament, the word 'blessing' is the Greek word *eulogia*, from which we get the word 'eulogy'. So, in practice, this means 'to speak well of' or 'speak the intention and favour of God' on a person.

That's the definition of blessing that I will use for this book. Blessing is to speak the intentions or favour of God over someone or some situation.

God, for the most part, in His wisdom, has decided to limit His work on earth to what He can accomplish through His people. This is how He brings His kingdom to earth. Accordingly, He wants us to bless on His behalf. So, as a Christian, I can speak God's intentions or favour over someone or some situation in the name of Jesus. If I do that with faith and love, then I have the power of heaven behind what I say, and I can expect that God will move to change things from where they are, to where He wants them to be. When I bless someone intentionally, with love and faith, I enable God to activate His plans for that person.

On the other hand, someone may purposefully, or usually inadvertently, speak the intentions of Satan over someone, or even themselves, which then enables demonic forces to activate their plans for that person – that is, to steal, kill and destroy. But praise God,

> *He who is in you is greater than he who is in the world (1 John 4:4).*

It is the very heart of God to bless – indeed His very nature! God's desire to bless is shockingly extravagant. Nothing can stop Him. He is determined to bless humankind. His longing is that Jesus will have many brothers and sisters. That's us! Yet, while it is the very heart of God to bless humankind, He desires even more that His people will bless one another.

When we bless in Jesus' name, the Holy Spirit comes because we are reflecting something that the Father is doing – we are speaking the words that the Father desires to be said. I am constantly amazed at how true this is. When I bless someone, the Holy Spirit is involved – He touches the other person, love is released and things change. Often people hug me afterwards, or they weep and say, 'You don't know how timely and powerful that was', or 'You don't know how much I needed that'.

But here is something very important to note: we bless from a place of intimacy with God, from His presence. Our spiritual proximity with God is all-important. Our words are His words and they are anointed with His power to accomplish His intentions for that person or situation. But let's back up a bit…

OUR SPIRITUAL AUTHORITY

In the Old Testament, the priests were to intercede for the people and to pronounce blessings over them.

This is the way you shall bless the children of Israel. Say to them:

The Lord bless you and keep you;
The Lord make His face to shine upon you,
and be gracious to you.
The Lord lift up His countenance upon you,
and give you peace.

So shall they put My name upon the children of Israel, and I will bless them. (Numbers 6:23-27)

In the New Testament, we as Christians are called:

a chosen generation, a royal priesthood, a holy nation, His own special people, that you may proclaim the praises of Him who called you out of darkness into His marvellous light. (1 Peter 2:9)

And Jesus

…has made us kings and priests to His God and Father… (Revelation 1:6)

Some time ago, I was sitting on Ouen Toro, a lookout point in Noumea, seeking a message to bring to a prayer group. I sensed God say, 'You don't know who you are.' Then some months later: 'If you only knew the authority you have in Christ Jesus you would change the world.' Both of these messages were for particular groups of people but, I realised later, they were for me too.

I think it is generally known in Christian circles that speaking directly to a disease or condition (a 'mountain' – Mark 11:23) and commanding a healing is more effective than asking God to do it (Matthew 10:8; Mark 16:17-18). This has certainly been my experience and the experience of many other well-known and respected people active and successful in the healing and deliverance ministry. I believe that Jesus says in effect, '*You* heal the sick (in my name). It's not *My* job, it's *your* job. *You do it.*'

God wants to heal and He wants to do it through us. God wants to deliver and He wants to do it through us. God wants to bless and He wants to do it through us. We can ask *God* to bless, or *we* can bless in Jesus' name.

Some years ago, I remember taking the time to go early to work to bless my business. I started with, 'God, bless Colmar Brunton.' It felt flat. Then I changed – a little timidly at first – from 'God bless Colmar Brunton' to:

> *Colmar Brunton, I bless you in the name of*
> *the Father, the Son and the Holy Spirit.*
> *I bless you in Auckland, and I bless you in*
> *Wellington, and I bless you in the regions.*
> *I bless you at work and I bless you at home.*
> *I release the Kingdom of God in this place.*
> *Come Holy Spirit, You are welcome here.*
> *I release love and joy and peace and patience*
> *and kindness and goodness and gentleness*
> *and faithfulness and self-control and unity.*

In the name of Jesus, I release ideas from
the Kingdom of God that would help our clients
succeed and make the world a better place.
I release favour in the client marketplace.
I release favour in the employment marketplace.
I bless our vision: 'Better Business, Better World'.
In Jesus' name, amen.

As I felt led, I would make a sign of the cross at our entrance and spiritually apply the protection of the blood of Jesus over our business.

From the moment I changed from 'God bless Colmar Brunton' to 'I bless Colmar Brunton in the name of the Father, the Son and the Holy Spirit', the anointing of God fell on me – I was feeling God's pleasure and affirmation. It was like He was saying, 'You've got it, son; that's what I want you to do.' Though I must have done this now hundreds of times, I've always felt God's pleasure in it. And the results? The atmosphere in the office changed, and changed rapidly, to the point where people would openly talk about it, and wonder why things were so different. It really was amazing! Blessing really can change our world.

But I didn't stop there. In the morning, while the office was still empty, when I came to the chair of someone who needed wisdom for a particular situation, I would bless them, laying hands on the chair, believing that an anointing to accomplish the blessing would pass into the fabric of the chair and so onto the person sitting on it (Acts 19:12). Whenever I was aware of specific needs people faced, I would bless in that manner.

I particularly remember a person who habitually blasphemed – that is, he used God's name as an expletive. One morning I laid hands on his chair, binding the spirit of blasphemy, in Jesus' name. It took several goes, but eventually the evil spirit behind it had to bow the knee to a greater power and blasphemy disappeared from the man's workplace vocabulary.

I also remember a man coming to me for prayer, wanting God to take him out of his place of work because everyone there was blaspheming. I took a contrary view: this man was there to bless his workplace and change the atmosphere! We can change our world.

I have formed the view that while God desires to bless humankind, even more He desires for us – His people, His kids – to bless humankind. You have spiritual authority. *You bless!*

Our heavenly Father wants us to *participate*, to *co-labour*, with Him in His redemptive work. We can bless humankind with healing and deliverance but we can also bless humankind with our words. We are the people God uses to bless the world. What a privilege and responsibility!

So, for me, blessing is speaking God's purposes over people's lives or situations with love, eyes open, intentionally, with authority and power, out of our Holy-Spirit-filled spirit. Simply put, blessing is acting in faith by declaring God's intention for the person or situation. When we declare God's intention, we release His ability to change things from where they are to where He wants them to be.

And remember – we are blessed because we bless.

PART TWO:

How to Do It

SOME IMPORTANT PRINCIPLES

Make a Clean Mouth a Lifestyle

> *And so blessing and cursing come pouring out of the same mouth. Surely my brothers and sisters this is not right! (James 3:10, NLB)*

> *If you utter what is precious and not what is worthless, you shall be as my mouth. (Jeremiah 15:19b, RSV)*

If you want to speak God's intentions over people, then you need to avoid speaking words that are worthless – or worse than worthless.

Ask the Holy Spirit What to Say
Stir up your spirit (through worship or speaking in tongues). Ask the Holy Spirit to let you sense the

Father's love for the person you want to bless. Pray something like this:

> *Father, what do you desire to be said? Please give me a word of blessing for this person. How can I encourage or comfort him or her?*

Blessing as Distinct from Intercession

Most people find that it is quite difficult to learn to speak out blessings. Invariably they start to 'intercede', asking the Father to bless. Although this is a good thing to do, a blessing spoken in this way is actually a prayer, and it is important to know the difference. Speaking or pronouncing blessings does not replace prayer and intercession, but is a companion to them – they should be regularly found together.

The authors Roy Godwin and Dave Roberts in their book *The Grace Outpouring* put this very well:

> *When we bless, we look the person in the eye (if that is the situation) and speak directly to him*

or her. For instance, we may say something like, 'I bless you in the name of the Lord, that the grace of the Lord Jesus might rest upon you. I bless you in His name that the Father's love might surround you and fill you; that you may know in your deepest being just how fully and completely He accepts you and rejoices over you.'

Notice the personal pronoun 'I'. It is I who is pronouncing blessing in the name of Jesus over the person directly. I have not prayed to God for a blessing but have spoken a blessing using the authority Jesus gives us to pronounce blessing on the people so that He may come and bless them.

Don't Judge

Don't judge whether someone deserves a blessing or not. True blessing, spoken over someone or something, describes the way God sees them. God's focus is not on how they may appear to be at the moment, but rather the way they are supposed to be.

For example, God called Gideon a *'mighty man of valour'* (Judges 6:12) when, at the time, he was anything but! Jesus called Peter a *'rock'* (Matthew 16:18) before he had the 'shoulders' to carry other people's dependence upon him. Further, we read, *'God … gives life to the dead, and calls those things which do not exist as though they did'* (Romans 4:17). If we understand this, it will eliminate our tendency to act as 'judge' on whether someone deserves a blessing.

The less people *deserve* blessing, the more they need it. People who bless non-deserving people receive the greatest blessing in return.

An Example to Illustrate

Imagine there is a man named Fred who has a problem with drinking. Fred's wife is not happy with him, so perhaps she'll pray something like: *'God bless Fred. Make him give up drinking and listen to me.'* But it would be far more powerful to say something like:

> *Fred, I bless you in Jesus' name. May God's plans for your life come to pass. May you become the*

man, the husband and father that God purposed for you to be. I bless you with freedom from addiction. I bless you with the peace of Christ.

The first blessing delegates the problem to God. It takes no effort – it's lazy. It's also judgemental and self-righteous, and focuses on Fred's sins.

The second blessing requires more thought and more love. It's not judgemental and it focuses on Fred's potential rather than his present state. Recently I heard someone say that Satan knows our name and potential but calls us by our sin, while God knows our sin but calls us by our real name and potential. The second blessing is more in keeping with God's plans and purposes. It reflects the redemptive heart of God. Remember, God loves Fred.

DIFFERENT SITUATIONS
WE MAY FACE

I am a student of blessing. When I started, I didn't know how to bless and I didn't find much to help me. I quite quickly began to realise that there are many different kinds of situations, so I want to offer you the suggestions that follow. You can adapt these to the needs of your particular situation, and according to what you believe the Holy Spirit wants you to say. This will take practice, but it's worth it.

Blessing Those Who Revile or Curse You
Many years ago, an employee who had recently resigned came round to my house for a coffee and to say goodbye. Her beliefs were along New Age lines – the 'goddess within', and the like. During the conversation, she said that the last two companies she had worked for, and left, had subsequently gone

broke. I hadn't been a Christian very long at that time, but even so I recognised her words were a curse looking to alight. I felt a few seconds of fear and then, in my mind, I refused to accept it. But I didn't go the extra step of blessing her. After asking her permission to pray what was on my heart, I could have said something like:

> *Deborah (not her real name), I bind the influence of witchcraft in your life. I bless you in Jesus' name. I declare the goodness of God over you. May God's intentions for your life come to pass … I bless your gifts, may they bless your future employer and bring glory to God. May you become the wonderful woman of God that He intends you to be. In Jesus' name, amen.*

Blessing Those Who Hurt or Reject You
I once prayed for a woman who was struggling emotionally and financially after her husband had left her. I asked her if she could forgive him. Well that was hard but, to her credit, she did it. Then I asked her if

she could bless her husband. She was a bit shocked, but willing to give it a go. Even though her husband wasn't present, I led her along the lines of:

> *I bless you my husband. May all of God's plans for your life and our marriage come to fruition. May you become the man, the husband and the father that God intends for you to be. May God's grace and favour be with you. In Jesus' name, amen.*

It was awkward to begin with, but then she caught the Father's heart and God's anointing fell. We both wept as the Holy Spirit ministered to her and, I believe, to her husband as well. God's ways are not our ways.

To bless in these types of situations is so courageous – majestic, even – and Christlike.

Blessing the undeserving is God's heart – His speciality, so to speak. Consider the thief who was crucified alongside Jesus, or the woman caught in adultery. What about you and me?

Blessing is 'unworldly' and counter-intuitive – it's not something that people in hurtful situations feel naturally inclined to do. But it's God's way, and it can heal the one doing the blessing as well as the one receiving the blessing. It cuts off the toxic squirt of bitterness, revenge, resentment and anger, which might otherwise harm your body and shorten your life.

Here is an email I recently received from Denis:

About three months ago I was speaking to my brother on the phone. We don't communicate much as he lives and works in another city.

As we were about to finish our friendly chat, I asked him if he would allow me to bless the business that he ran with his wife. He didn't respond well. He was very rude and said some things that really upset me, and I wondered if our relationship was permanently damaged. However, in the days and weeks that followed, as I went about my daily life, I used the principles of the awesome power of blessing to speak God's favour on my brother's business. Sometimes I did this two to three times a day. Then, three months later, the day before Christmas, my brother rang me as if nothing had happened. I was quite amazed at his very friendly attitude and there was no resentment between us at all.

The awesome power of blessing of circumstances outside our control really works… Praise the Lord!

Blessing Those Who Have Provoked You

One of the most infuriating things for some of us is when people do selfish, inconsiderate or downright cheating things in traffic. It happens all the time. Unchristian words can spring to mind and come out of our mouths in a flash. When this happens, we are cursing someone who was made by God and whom God loves. God may very well defend that person.

Next time this happens, try blessing the other motorist, instead of speaking angry words:

I bless that young man who cut in on me (cheated on the queue). I declare Your love over him, Lord. I release Your goodness over him and all Your intentions for his life. I bless this young man and I call forth his potential. May he get safely home and be a blessing to his family. In Jesus' name, amen.

Or less formally:

Father, I bless the driver of that car, in Jesus' name. May your love pursue him and overtake him and arrest him!

One of my readers made an interesting observation:

The thing that I have noticed is that blessing has changed me. I can't bless people that have irritated me, for example, and then speak – or even think – wrong thoughts about them. That would be wrong. Instead I am looking for good results to come from the blessing… – Jillian

I once had a friend named John who invited me to pray over a family dispute concerning an inheritance. The dispute was dragging on and getting increasingly unpleasant. I suggested that instead of praying, we bless the situation.

> *We bless this situation of dispute over this inheritance in Jesus' name. We come against division, contention and strife and we loose justice and fairness and reconciliation. As we bless this situation, we put aside our own thoughts and desires and we release God to activate His purposes for the division of the inheritance. In Jesus' name, amen.*

Within a couple of days the matter was amicably resolved.

I love what another of my readers had to say:

> *I have been taken aback by the fast 'response time' that I have seen in blessing others. It's as if the Lord is ready to lunge out in love towards people if we will but release the prayers of blessing on them. – Pastor Darin Olson, Junction City, Oregon Nazarene Church*

Blessing really can change our world.

BLESSING, INSTEAD OF CURSING, OURSELVES

Recognising and Breaking Curses

How common are these thoughts: 'I'm ugly, I'm dumb, I'm clumsy, I'm slow-witted, no one likes me, God could never use me, I'm a sinner…'? There are so many lies that Satan causes us to believe.

I have a friend who does this all the time, and it saddens me. 'Oh, you silly girl, Rose (not her real name). You've messed up again. You can't do anything right…'

Don't repeat or accept these curses! Instead, bless yourself.

I remember a particular prayer group situation. I discerned a spirit of worthlessness over a lady who had come to be prayed for. In the course of praying, she said, 'I'm dumb.' I asked her where she had heard that.

She told me her parents had said it over her. How sad … and how common.

I guided her along these lines:

> *In Jesus' name, I forgive my parents. I forgive myself. I break the words my parents and I spoke over me. I have the mind of Christ. I am smart.*

We summarily dismissed the spirits of rejection and worthlessness, and then I blessed her and declared over her that she was God's princess, that she was valuable to Him, that God was going to use her to bless others, to bring emotional healing and hope to others. I blessed her with boldness.

Slowly she absorbed this blessing. She started to shine. The following week she recounted how much good it had done her. We really can change our world.

Anyone can do this. The Bible is full of God's intentions for people and we can declare these intentions over them.

I'd like to share another example. I prayed for a lady recently who had stomach pain. As I prayed, the Holy Spirit fell on her and she doubled over as demons left her. All was well for a few days and then the pain returned. 'Why, Lord?' she asked. She sensed the Holy Spirit remind her that some time earlier, while she was at a camp, someone had said to her to make sure she cooked the chicken properly or people would get sick. She replied that she didn't want to be sick over the next few days (the duration of the conference), but after that it wouldn't matter. She had to break the power of those careless words, and then she immediately regained her healing.

Blessing One's Mouth

I bless my mouth to utter what is precious and not what is worthless, and to be as the Lord's mouth. (Based on Jeremiah 15:19)

Many of Jesus' miracles were accomplished just by speaking. For example, *'Go your way; your son lives'*

(John 4:50). I want that. That's why I bless my mouth and guard what comes out of it.

My wife and I were once staying at a hotel in Noumea. We could hear a baby crying almost incessantly throughout the night. After a couple of nights of this, my wife went out onto the adjoining deck and asked the mother what was wrong. The woman didn't know but said that the doctor had the baby on its third lot of antibiotics and nothing was working. My wife asked her if I could pray for the baby and she agreed, albeit sceptically. So in my very average French, I prayed for the baby and spoke in faith over the child, that she would 'sleep like a baby'. And she did.

Blessing One's Mind

I frequently say,

> *I bless my mind; I have the mind of Christ. Therefore I think His thoughts. May my mind be a holy place where the Holy Spirit is pleased to dwell. May it receive words of knowledge and wisdom and revelation.*

From time to time, I struggle with the purity of my thoughts, and I find this helps. I also bless my imagination, that it may be used for good and not for evil. I was having some difficulty with my imagination the other day – it was wandering into all sorts of places I didn't want it to go – and God impressed on me, '*See in your imagination Jesus doing His miracles … then see yourself doing them.*' I have found it much more effective to think about something good (Philippians 4:8) rather than thinking about not thinking about something! And blessing your own mind and imagination helps greatly in achieving the goal of holiness.

Once when I was feeling down about a failure in my thought-life, the words of an old hymn bubbled up in my heart:

> *Be thou my vision, O Lord of my heart*
> *Naught be all else to me save that Thou art*
> *Thou my best thought by day or by night*
> *Waking or sleeping, Thy Presence my light.*

Blessing Our Bodies

Are you familiar with the verse: *'A merry heart does good, like a medicine'* (Proverbs 17:22)? The Bible is saying that our bodies respond to positive words and thoughts:

> *I bless my body. Today I break infirmity off myself.*
> *I bless my physical well-being.*

I once watched a video about a man who had a serious heart problem. His bypass had become blocked. He blessed his arteries for about three months, declaring them to be fearfully and wonderfully made. On returning to the doctor, it was discovered that he had miraculously had a new bypass!

I thought I would try this for my skin. I had a problem with sun damage from my youth. Now in my old age, little growths would come up on my shoulders and back, needing to be frozen off every few months. I decided to bless my skin. At first I just blessed it in Jesus' name. But then I read something about the nature of skin which changed my perspective. I realised that, although I was covered with it, I didn't know much about the largest organ in my body. I had talked *about* it, but I had never talked *to* it. And I doubt I had said anything nice about it – instead I complained. I was ungrateful.

But skin is amazing. It is an air-conditioning and sanitation system. It shields the body from invading germs and it heals itself. It covers and protects all our inner parts and does so beautifully.

> *Thank God for skin – wrinkles and all. Bless you, skin.*

After several months of this kind of blessing, my skin is now almost healed, but the key was when I began to appreciate and be thankful for it. It is fearfully and wonderfully made. A real lesson indeed. Complaining repulses the Kingdom of God; thankfulness attracts it.

Here is a testimony from my friend, David Goodman:

> *Some months ago I heard Richard preach on the subject of blessing – a somewhat innocuous subject, but one that resonated because of the angle*

from which it came. The upshot was that bless-ing need not be something we ask God for, but that we as Christians have the authority, if not responsibility, to take out into this fallen world and, as Christ's ambassadors, make an impact on the lives of other individuals for the Kingdom of God. We can go out and bless them in their lives, and reveal Christ to them at the same time.

The idea is fine when one is considering others, but this idea struck a brick wall for me when I had to consider blessing myself. I could not shake off the notion that I was not worthy, that I was being selfish, that I was taking God for granted. My ideas changed when I saw that we, as Christians, are a new creation, born again and created for a purpose that God has planned for us. That being so, the body we have now is one that we should treasure and take care of – we are now, after all, a temple for the dwelling of the Holy Spirit.

That said, I started a short experiment – each day I would wake, I would bless a part of my body, thank it for its performance; praise it for a job well done. I would praise my fingers for their dexterity, for the skills they have in doing all the tasks required of them and more. I would praise and thank my legs for the tireless job of transportation and speed, for their ability to work in unison. I praised my body for all parts working well together. One odd thing came out of this.

Because I felt so much better physically and mentally, I turned my thoughts to that of a pain that I had had for some months in my lower arm – a pain that seemed to be in the bone and which needed to be rubbed regularly to at least partially relieve the constant throbbing. I focused on this area, praising my body for its healing abilities, for its tenacity to overcome those things that are thrown against it, for the support that other parts could give while repairs could be made to another. It was only about three weeks later that I woke one morning and realised that I no longer felt any pain in my arm; that the ache had entirely vanished and has not returned.

I came to realise that while there is surely a time

and place for the gift of healing to be exercised through faith for the benefit of others, there is also another avenue open to us as individuals to engage the gift of healing in ourselves. It is a lesson in humility, that we can trust what God has given to our new bodies, that we can go forth in confidence in a new and living way of life.

Blessing Your Home, Marriage and Children

Your House – Typical House Blessing

It is a good idea to bless your house and to renew that blessing at least once a year. Blessing the place where you live simply involves using your spiritual authority in Christ Jesus to dedicate and consecrate that place to the Lord. It is inviting the Holy Spirit to come, and compelling everything else that is not of God to leave.

A home is not just bricks and mortar – it has personality too. Just as you have legal access to your house now, someone else had legal access to it, or your property, before you. Things may have happened in that place that brought either blessings or curses. No matter what happened, it is *your* authority that determines what the spiritual atmosphere will be like from now on. If there is demonic activity still going on from past ownership, you will likely sense it – and it is up to you to drive these forces out.

Of course, you have to consider what demonic forces you may be unwittingly giving access to your home yourself. Do you have ungodly paintings, artefacts, books, music or DVDs? What TV programmes do you allow in? Is there sin in your home?

Here is a simple blessing you could make as you walk through your house room by room:

I bless this house, our home. I declare that this house belongs to God, I consecrate it to God and place it under the Lordship of Jesus Christ. It is a house of blessing.

I break every curse in this house with the blood of Jesus. I take authority over any and every demon in Jesus' name and I command them to leave now and never to return. I cast out every spirit of strife, division and discord. I cast out the spirit of poverty.

Come Holy Spirit and evict everything that is not of You. Fill this house with Your presence. Let Your fruit come: love, joy, peace, kindness, patience, goodness, gentleness, faithfulness and self-control. I bless this house with overflowing peace and abounding love. May all who come here sense Your presence and be blessed. In Jesus' name, amen.

I have walked around the boundary of my property, blessing it and spiritually applying the blood of Jesus Christ for the protection of the property, and the people within it, from every evil and from natural disasters.

Your Marriage

We have the kind of marriage we bless or we have the kind of marriage we curse.

When I first read this statement in *The Power of Blessing* by Kerry Kirkwood, I was a bit shocked. Is this true?

I've given it a lot of thought, and I believe that these words are largely true – any unhappiness with our marriage or our children is due to us not blessing them! By blessing, we receive God's intended goodness towards us in full measure – including long life and healthy relationships. We become partakers, or partners, with what and whom we are blessing.

Watch out for curses. Husbands and wives know each other so well. We know all the hot buttons. Do you say anything like this? Are these kinds of things ever said over you? 'You never listen', 'Your memory is terrible'. 'You can't cook', 'You're hopeless at…' If said often enough, these kinds of words become curses and become true.

Don't curse, bless. Remember, if you curse (speak death words) you will not inherit the blessing God wants for you. Worse than that, cursing affects *us* more than the one we may be cursing. Could that be one reason why prayers are not answered?

Learning to bless can be like learning a new language – awkward at first. For example,

> *Nicole, I bless you in the name of the Father, the Son and the Holy Spirit. I release all of God's goodness over you. May God's intentions for your life come to fruition.*

> *I bless your gift of meeting and loving people, your gift of warm hospitality. I bless your gift of making people feel at ease. I declare that you are God's hostess, that you receive people as He would. I bless you with energy to keep doing this even in your latter years. I bless you with health and long life. I bless you with the oil of joy.*

Your Children

There are many ways to bless a child. Here's how I bless my granddaughter, who is four years old:

> *Ashley, I bless your life. May you become a*

wonderful woman of God. I bless your mind to remain sound and for you to have wisdom and discernment in all decisions. I bless your body to remain pure until marriage and to be healthy and strong. I bless your hands and feet to do the work that God has planned for you to do. I bless your mouth. May it speak words of truth and encouragement. I bless your heart to be true to the Lord. I bless your husband-to-be and your future children's lives with richness and unity. I love everything about you, Ashley, and I am proud to be your papa.

Of course, where a child is struggling in some area we can bless them appropriately. If they find it difficult to learn at school, we can bless their minds to remember lessons and to understand the concepts behind the teaching; if they are being bullied, we can bless them to grow in wisdom and stature and in favour with God and other children; and so on.

I remember speaking with a wonderful woman of God about her grandson. Everything she said about him focussed on his faults, his rebellious attitude, and the behavioural problems he was having at school. He had been sent to a camp to help get him on the straight and narrow, and had been sent home again because he was so disruptive.

After listening for a while, I suggested to the woman that she was inadvertently cursing her grandson through the way she was speaking about him, and that she was imprisoning him with her words. So she stopped speaking negatively, and instead she intentionally blessed him. Her husband, the boy's grandfather, did the same. Within a matter of days, the boy had completely changed, returning to the camp and flourishing. Talk about a quick response to the awesome power of blessing!

One of the most wonderful things that a father can give his children is a father's blessing. I learnt about this from *The Father's Blessing* by Frank Hammond, which is a wonderful book. Without a father's blessing there is always a sense of something missing – a void is created that nothing else can fill. Fathers, lay hands on your children, and other family members, (e.g. place your hand on their head or shoulders) and bless them often. Discover the good things God will do for both you and them.

Wherever I share this message, I ask adult men and women, 'How many people here have ever had their father lay hands on them and bless them?' Very few people raise their hands. Then I turn the question around: 'How many people here have *never* had their father lay hands on them and bless them?' Almost everyone raises their hand.

Then I ask if they would allow me to be a spiritual father to them in that moment – a substitute – so that I might, in the power of the Holy Spirit, bless them with the blessing they never had. The response has been overwhelming: tears, deliverance, joy, healing. Just amazing!

If you yearn for a father's blessing, as I did, then say the following out loud over yourself. It is a blessing that I have adapted from Frank Hammond's book.

A Father's Blessing

My child, I love you! You are special. You are a gift from God. I thank God for allowing me to be a father to you. I am proud of you and I rejoice over you. And now I bless you.

I bless you with the healing of all wounds of the heart – wounds of rejection, neglect and abuse that you have suffered. In Jesus' name, I break the power of all cruel and unjust words spoken over you.

I bless you with overflowing peace, the peace that only the Prince of Peace can give.

I bless your life with fruitfulness: good fruit, abundant fruit and fruit that remains.

I bless you with success. You are the head and not the tail; you are above and not beneath.

I bless the gifts that God has given you. I bless you with wisdom to make good decisions and to develop your full potential in Christ.

I bless you with overflowing prosperity, enabling you to be a blessing to others.

I bless you with spiritual influence, for you are the light of the world and the salt of the earth.

I bless you with depth of spiritual understanding and a close walk with your Lord. You will not stumble or falter, for the Word of God will be a lamp to your feet and a light to your path.

I bless you to see women/men as Jesus did and does.

I bless you to see, draw out and celebrate the gold in people, not the dirt.

I bless you to release God in the workplace – not just to testify, or model good character, but also to glorify God with the excellence and creativity of your work.

I bless you with good friends. You have favour with God and man.

I bless you with abounding and overflowing love, from which you will minister God's grace to others. You will minister God's comforting grace to others. You are blessed, my child! You are blessed with all spiritual blessings in Christ Jesus. Amen!

Testimonies of the Value of a Father's Blessing

I was changed by the father's blessing. Since I was born I had never heard such a message preached. I have never had a biological father to speak into my life up to where I am now. God used you, Richard, to bring me to a point where I needed to pray and have a spiritual father declare a father's blessings on my life. When you released a father-to-son blessing, my heart was comforted and now I am happy and blessed. – Pastor Wycliffe Alumasa, Kenya

It had been a long and difficult journey navigating my way through depression; a battle fought on many fronts – mind, spirit, body. Healing my past ended up being key and nothing was a more significant step forward than forgiving my father – not only for the hurtful things he had done in the past but more so for the things he hadn't done – his omissions. My father never told me he loved me. He had an emotional block. He couldn't find loving, caring, emotional words to say – despite a craving in my soul to hear them.

Whilst through the forgiveness and inner healing journey my depression lifted, I still carried some physical symptoms – the biggest being irritable bowel syndrome. I had been prescribed drugs and a diet from my doctor with some but little effect, which I was told were to manage the symptoms, as opposed to providing a remedy.

A friend of mine, Richard, had been telling me stories about the father's blessing, and what responses people had. Something in my spirit caught hold of the idea. I became aware of the fact that while I had forgiven my father for the gap he left, I hadn't actually filled the gap or satisfied my soul's craving.

And so it happened. One morning in a café, over breakfast, Richard stepped into the shoes my father couldn't fill and blessed me as a son. The Holy Spirit fell on me and remained with me that entire day. It was a beautiful experience and that part of my soul which had been crying out was at peace.

An unexpected outcome however was that my symptoms of irritable bowel syndrome stopped completely. My medication and the doctor's diet were thrown out. When my soul received what it had been craving, my body was healed too.
– Ryan

Blessing Others by Releasing the Prophetic

Although I have given examples to help you get started, it is good to ask the Holy Spirit to help you be like God's mouth, declaring and releasing God's specific intention or a 'word in season' (the right word at the right time). If the situation permits, activate your spirit with praying in tongues or worship.

You may start by using the various models above, but trust that the Holy Spirit will direct you. Listen to His heartbeat. You may start haltingly, but you will soon catch the heart of the Lord.

Blessing Your Workplace

Turn back to Part 1 and adapt the example I gave, from my own experience, to your circumstances. Be open to what God shows you – He may adjust your perspective. Blessing is not some kind of magic spell. For example, God will not make people buy what they don't need or want. Nor will God bless laziness and dishonesty. But if you meet His conditions, then you should bless your business – that God would help you to take it from where it is now to where He wants it to be. Listen for His counsel or the counsel of people He sends to you. Be open. But also expect His favour, because He loves you and wants you to succeed.

I received the following testimony from Ben Fox:

> *My particular job in the property industry underwent changes in the last few years and there*

had been a significant downturn in my business. I had gone to several people to pray for my job because my workload was declining to the point where I was worried and anxious.

About the same time, in early 2015, I heard Mr Brunton preach a series of messages about blessing one's job, business, family and other areas. Until that time, the focus of my prayers had been to ask God to help me in these areas. The idea of ourselves speaking a blessing had not been taught to me, but I can now see that it is written throughout the Bible, and I know that God calls us, and has given us the authority, to do so in the name of Jesus. So I started to bless my work – to speak the word of God over it and to thank God for it. I persisted with blessing my work each morning and also thanking God for new business, asking Him to send me clients whom I could help.

Over the next twelve months, my work volume increased significantly and, since then, at times I have been hard-pressed to handle the amount of work that has come my way. I have learned that there is a way to include God in our everyday vocations, and blessing our work is part of what God calls us to do. I therefore give God all the credit. I also began to invite the Holy Spirit into my workday, asking for wisdom and creative ideas. In particular, I have noticed that when I ask the Holy Spirit to help me with the efficiency of my work, I usually finish it well before the expected time.

It appears to me that the teaching of the blessing, and how to do it, has been forgotten by many churches, as other Christians I talk to are not aware of it. Blessing my work has now become a daily habit, as has blessing others. I also look forward with expectation to seeing the fruit in the people and the things I bless when it is in accordance with God's Word and in Jesus' name.

Blessing a Community

I am thinking here of a church – or similar organisation – blessing the community in which it operates.

People of .... (community), we bless you in the name of Jesus to know God, to know His purposes for your lives, and to know His blessings on each one of you, your families and all the situations of your lives.

We bless every household in .... (community). We bless every marriage and we bless the relationships between family members of different generations.

We bless your health and your wealth.

We bless the work of your hands. We bless every wholesome enterprise you're involved with. May they prosper.

We bless the pupils at your schools; we bless them to learn and to understand what they are taught. May they grow in wisdom and in stature and in favour with God and man. We bless the teachers and pray that school may be a safe and wholesome place, where belief in God and in Jesus can be comfortably taught.

We speak to the hearts of all the people who are in this community. We bless them to be open to the wooing of the Holy Spirit and to become more and more responsive to the voice of God. We bless them with the overspill of the Kingdom of Heaven that we experience here at .... (church).

Obviously this type of blessing should be customised for the particular type of community. If it is a farming community, you might bless the land and the animals; if it's a community where unemployment is common, then bless local businesses to create jobs. Target the blessing to the need. Don't worry about whether they deserve it or not! People will sense in their hearts where the blessing has come from.

Blessing the Land

In Genesis, we see God blessing humankind, giving them dominion over the land and all living things, and commanding them to be fruitful and to multiply. This was an aspect of humankind's original glory.

When I was in Kenya recently, I met a missionary who took in street kids and taught them about agriculture. He told me the story of a Muslim community who claimed that their land was cursed, because nothing would grow on it. My missionary friend and his Christian community blessed the land and it became fertile. This was a dramatic demonstration of God's power released by blessing.

While in Kenya, I also walked all around the orphanage our church supported, blessing their orchard, their garden, their chooks and their cows. (I have blessed my own fruit trees with great results.)

Geoff Wiklund tells a story of a church in the Philippines that blessed a piece of church land in the midst of a serious drought. Their land was the only place that received rain. Neighbouring farmers came to gather water for their rice from the ditches that surrounded the perimeter of the church land. This is another remarkable miracle in which God's favour was released through blessing.

Blessing the Lord

Although I have left this to last, it should really come first. The reason I put it last, however, is because it doesn't seem to fit the model of 'speaking the intentions or favour of God over someone or something'. Rather, it is the idea of 'making happy'.

How do we bless God? One way of doing this is demonstrated in Psalm 103:

> *Bless the Lord O my soul ... and forget not all His benefits...*

What are the Lord's benefits towards our souls? He forgives, heals, redeems, crowns, satisfies, renews...

I make it a practice to remember and thank God every day for what He does in and through me. I remember and appreciate all that He is for me. This blesses Him, and me too! How do you feel when a child thanks or appreciates you for something you've done or said? It warms your heart and makes you want to do more for them.

A Final Word from a Reader

It is hard to explain how blessing has transformed my life. In my brief experience so far, no one has turned down a blessing when I have offered to give one – I even had the chance to bless a Muslim man. Offering to pray a blessing over a person's life opens a door ... it is such a simple, non-threatening way to bring the Kingdom of God into a situation, into a person's life. For me, being able to pray a blessing has added a very special tool to my spiritual tool kit... it's like a part of my life was previously missing and has now been slotted into place... – Sandi

APPLICATIONS

- Think of someone who has hurt you – forgive if necessary, but then go further and bless them.

- Consider things you say regularly where you curse others or yourself. What are you going to do about it?

- Write out a blessing for yourself, your spouse, and your children.

- Meet with another person and be open to prophesy over them. Ask God for the revelation of something specific and encouraging for that person. Start with speaking in general terms, for example, 'I bless you in the name of Jesus. May God's plans and purposes for your life come to fruition…' and wait, be patient. Remember you have the mind of Christ. Then swap over, and have the other person prophetically bless you.

- In your church, construct a corporate blessing to outreach and heal your region, or bless the mission you already have.

HOW TO BECOME
A CHRISTIAN

This little book was written for Christians. By 'Christians', I don't just mean people who live good lives. I mean people who are 'born again' by the Spirit of God and who love and follow Jesus Christ.

People are made in three parts: spirit, soul and body. The spirit part was designed to know and commune with a holy God, who is Spirit. Humans were made for intimacy with God, spirit to Spirit. However, human sin separates us from God, resulting in the death of our spirit and loss of communion with God.

Consequently, people tend to operate out of their souls and bodies only. The soul comprises the intellect, the will and the emotions. The result of this is only too apparent in the world: selfishness, pride, greed, hunger, wars, and lack of true peace and meaning.

But God had a plan to redeem humankind. God the Father sent His Son, Jesus, who is also God, to come to earth as a man to show us what God was like – *'if you have seen Me you have seen the Father'* – and to take upon Himself the consequences of our sin. His horrible death on the cross was planned from the very beginning and was predicted in detail in the Old Testament. He paid the price for humankind's sin. Divine justice was satisfied.

But then God raised Jesus from the dead. Jesus promises that those who believe in Him will also be raised from the dead to spend eternity with Him. He gives us His Spirit *now*, as a guarantee, so that we would know Him and walk with Him for the remainder of our earthly lives.

So there we have the essence of the gospel of Jesus Christ. If you acknowledge and confess your sin, if you believe that Jesus took your punishment upon Himself on the cross and that He was raised from the dead, then His righteousness will be imputed to you. God will send His Holy Spirit to regenerate your human spirit – that's what it means to be born again – and you will be able to begin to know and commune with God intimately – which is why He created you in the first place! When your physical body dies, Christ will raise you up and give you a glorious, imperishable one. Wow!

While you continue on this earth, the Holy Spirit (who is also God) will work *in* you (to clean you up and make you more like Jesus in character) and *through* you (to be a blessing to others).

Those who choose not to receive what Jesus paid for will go to judgement with all its consequences. You don't want that.

Here is a prayer you can pray. If you pray it sincerely you will be born again.

> *Dear God in heaven, I come to You in the name of Jesus. I acknowledge to You that I am a sinner. (Confess all your known sins.) I am truly sorry for my sins and the life that I have lived without You and I need Your forgiveness.*
>
> *I believe that Your only Son, Jesus Christ, shed*

His precious blood on the cross and died for my sins, and I am now willing to turn from my sin.

You said in the Bible (Romans 10:9) that if we declare that Jesus is Lord and believe in our hearts that God raised Jesus from the dead, we shall be saved.

Right now I confess Jesus as the Lord of my soul. I believe that God raised Jesus from the dead. This very moment I accept Jesus Christ as my own personal Saviour and, according to His Word, right now I am saved. Thank You, Lord, for loving me so much that You were willing to die in my place. You are amazing, Jesus, and I love you.

Now I ask You to help me by Your Spirit to be the person that You purposed for me to be from before the beginning of time. Lead me to fellow believers and the church of Your choice that I might grow in You. In Jesus' name, amen.